PRO WRESTLING LEGENDS

Steve Austin
The Story of the Wrestler They Call "Stone Cold"

Bill Goldberg

Ric Flair
The Story of the Wrestler They Call "The Nature Boy"

Mick Foley
The Story of the Wrestler They Call "Mankind"

Bret Hart
The Story of the Wrestler They Call "The Hitman"

Billy Kidman

Lex Luger
The Story of the Wrestler They Call "The Total Package"

Vince McMahon Jr.

Shawn Michaels
The Story of the Wrestler They Call "The Heartbreak Kid"

Kevin Nash

Pro Wrestling: The Early Years

Pro Wrestling's Greatest Matches

Pro Wrestling's Greatest Tag Teams

Pro Wrestling's Greatest Wars

Pro Wrestling's Most Punishing Finishing Moves

Randy Savage
The Story of the Wrestler They Call "Macho Man"

The Story of the Wrestler They Call "Chyna"

The Story of the Wrestler They Call "Diamond" Dallas Page

The Story of the Wrestler They Call "Hollywood" Hulk Hogan

The Story of the Wrestler They Call "The Rock"

The Story of the Wrestler They Call "Sting"

The Story of the Wrestler They Call "The Undertaker"

Jesse Ventura
The Story of the Wrestler They Call "The Body"

The Women of Pro Wrestling

CHELSEA HOUSE PUBLISHERS

The Story of the Wrestler They Call "Chyna"

Johanna Brindisi

Chelsea House Publishers
Philadelphia

Produced by Chestnut Productions and Choptank Syndicate, Inc.

Editor and Picture Researcher: Mary Hull
Design and Production: Lisa Hochstein

CHELSEA HOUSE PUBLISHERS

Editor in Chief: Sally Cheney
Associate Editor in Chief: Kim Shinners
Production Manager: Pamela Loos
Art Director: Sara Davis
Director of Photography: Judy L. Hasday

Cover Photos: Front: Jeff Eisenberg Sports Photography
and Howard Kernats

The Chelsea House World Wide Web site
address is http://www.chelseahouse.com

First Printing

1 3 5 7 9 8 6 4 2

Library of Congress Cataloging-in-Publication Data

Brindisi, Johanna.
      The story of the wrestler they call "Chyna" / Johanna Brindisi.
         p. cm. — (Pro wrestling legends)
      Includes bibliographical references.
      ISBN 0–7910–6442–5 (alk. paper) — ISBN 0–7910–6443–3 (pbk. : alk. paper)
         1. Laurer, Joanie, 1970– 2. Wrestlers—United States—Biography. 3. Women wrestlers—
      United States—Biography. I. Title. II. Series.

      GV1196.L38 B75 2001
      796.812'092—dc21
      [B]
                                                                                    2001017300

Contents

CHAPTER 1
REWRITING THE RECORD BOOKS   **7**

CHAPTER 2
HARD-KNOCK LIFE   **13**

CHAPTER 3
BIGGER AND BETTER THINGS   **19**

CHAPTER 4
THE WWF COMES CALLING   **31**

CHAPTER 5
A DAY IN THE LIFE OF A PRO WRESTLER   **41**

CHAPTER 6
BREAKING DOWN THE WALLS OF CHYNA   **49**

QUOTEWORTHY: Chyna on Chyna   **57**

Chronology   **61**

Further Reading   **62**

Index   **63**

1 REWRITING THE RECORD BOOKS

Throughout the ages, wrestling has been a man's sport. Until Joanie Laurer, aka Chyna, came along, few promoters had ever had the guts to put a woman in the same ring as a man. Their reluctance was part chauvinism and part reality. By nature men are usually two times stronger than women, and their egos usually bruise a lot faster than those of the ladies. Male wrestlers are constantly hitting the weights in the gym when they are not in the squared circle hitting their opponents. No promoter wanted to risk a lawsuit, a serious injury, or embarrassment, so none ever pursued such a crazy scenario.

In the past, there have been leading ladies in the ring like the Fabulous Moolah or Mae Young, but they grappled with other women wrestlers. They never dared to take on a man and they were never expected to. None of these women wrestlers had a muscular build like Laurer, nor did they have her determination to mix it up with the big boys.

For years people thought Laurer's dream of becoming a woman pro wrestler was crazy. After all, there weren't really any pro federations that allowed women wrestlers to make a lucrative living. And the idea of competing against men seemed impossible, not to mention risky. But Laurer didn't

Chyna holds the WWF Intercontinental belt and raises her arm in victory as she is declared the new WWF I-C champion on October 17, 1999. Chyna defeated Jeff Jarrett to become the first woman ever to hold a men's WWF championship.

7

Chyna smashes Jeff Jarrett with a trashcan during their match for the WWF Intercontinental title. The championship match was declared a "good housekeeping match," which meant the opponents could bring foreign objects into the ring and use them against one another.

listen to the nonbelievers. She just went about her business learning the wrestling ropes and taking advantage of every opportunity that came her way.

In the 1990s there were some popular women like Sable and Marlena on the World Wrestling Federation (WWF) circuit, but neither of these women were there for their wrestling skills. They were there mainly just for their looks. But Chyna wanted no part of the eye and arm candy roles assigned to women, who have long served as valets and managers in professional wrestling federations. She wanted a piece of the action.

Chyna first stepped on a WWF mat in the late 1990s as Triple H's bodyguard, protecting him from anyone who wanted a piece of wrestling's number one bad guy. She quickly branched out on her own on the WWF circuit, proving that she could more than handle herself against the opposite sex in the ring. She came on the scene with the intention of breaking down some barriers, and she was not afraid to break some bones in the male wrestling circuit on her way to respectability. The muscular bodybuilder did not want to be labeled as just a pretty lady in the ring; she wanted to kick some butt on the canvas.

Once Chyna put on her boots in the WWF, there wasn't anyone who was going to knock her off her professional wrestling feet. She didn't fit in at first, but when the federation's male talent realized she could handle herself on the squared circle, the talented rookie earned their respect.

"When I started, there was an incredible intimidation factor," Chyna told a reporter.

Chyna won the I-C belt from Jarrett after knocking him in the head with his guitar, rendering him unconscious.

"These guys were going to let a woman beat them up on TV? To get people to accept that I fight men as equal opponents—what a milestone!"

"When I first started in the WWF," Chyna explained on MTV's *Diary*, "Vince McMahon thought this was not going to work. People aren't used to seeing a woman like this. What's she going to do? Beat up on the guys? Their egos will be bruised."

But, soon enough, Chyna proved McMahon and all the other naysayers wrong.

And when given the opportunity, she didn't disappoint. "I have gone far beyond my expectations," she said. "I've done something so completely different. I've broken barriers. I don't want to have to ever depend on anybody else, and I want to be my own woman and have my own career."

And she wasn't going to let anyone or anything stop her, especially since she had been through hell as a child. So anything she endured on the mat could never compare to what she had to experience growing up. Wrestling men two times her size would be a piece of cake compared to her troubled childhood.

In 1999 Chyna became the first female wrestler to take part in both the Royal Rumble and the King of the Ring tournament. Even though she didn't win either event, it was an accomplishment just to be involved in these matches, as they were composed of some of the best male talent that the WWF had to offer.

On October 17, 1999, Chyna competed against WWF champion Jeff Jarrett at a No Mercy event in Cleveland, Ohio. She defeated Jarrett for the federation's intercontinental title, becoming the first woman ever to hold a men's WWF championship.

Chyna had come a long way in the WWF and more than proved herself inside the ropes. According to Laurer, "People don't even look at me as 'the woman' now. They just look at me as Chyna, one of the wrestlers." This is what Laurer wanted all along. She didn't want to be one of the guys, just one of the wrestlers. "I was a pioneer," Chyna said, "because I did what few women could ever do."

2 HARD-KNOCK LIFE

Chyna, the muscular wrestler known to grappling fans everywhere, was born Joanie Laurer in Rochester, New York, on December 27, 1970. It was a good thing she was born in the Big Apple, where only the strong survive, as she had to learn from a very young age how to overcome obstacles. The future WWF wrestler didn't have an easy childhood, as she came from a dysfunctional family.

In a March 2000 interview with *Raw* magazine, Laurer described her upbringing and the hard road she had to follow due to her unfortunate living circumstances. She said she was born to two people who didn't know how to raise a family. Some of the stories she told about her upbringing included her dad, who had a drinking problem.

"My earliest memories of my parents are very unhappy ones," Laurer said in the *Raw* interview. "My father drank for many years throughout my childhood. There were stories about him chasing my mother around the house with a butcher knife and stabbing her in the leg, or just picking up and leaving to hook up with other women."

Although Laurer came from a broken home, she had the determination to overcome her background. She had the will, drive, and desire to make something of herself. Another

As a teenager, Joanie Laurer found satisfaction through fitness training, but her bulging biceps only brought her ridicule. Though people once made fun of her muscular physique, today Chyna is a celebrated wrestler and public figure.

person might have been set back by such a difficult home life, but not this girl.

What bothered the young Laurer was that she was the product of two very well-educated people, who on paper should have made wonderful parents and had no problem raising a family. But unfortunately, this wasn't the case.

Laurer's mother was an executive for a large corporation, and her father was a highly successful businessman. But the sad fact was that her parents couldn't parlay their success in the workplace into success on the home front.

Laurer has described her mom as a "psycho co-dependent who had revolving-door marriages." "It seemed like I had a new stepfather every year," she said. "I always tried to accept them because I wanted another daddy."

"As a child, I wasn't necessarily athletic, but I was a ham," she said. "I was always dancing, singing, and dressing up in costumes—anything to be in the spotlight." The young and confused girl craved attention throughout her childhood and teen years. And then she started to do things to purposefully annoy her mom and stepfathers, like eating food they wanted to save, or even stealing and wearing her mom's jewelry.

Laurer's erratic behavior led her mother to believe her 15-year-old daughter was doing drugs, so she put Joanie in a rehab center. Almost immediately Laurer was discharged, as the counselors realized she was not a drug user or abuser. They did conclude that she was a very angry teen who needed some assistance.

Not long after her dismissal from the rehab center, Laurer turned to her father, who had since remarried and stopped drinking, for

Chyna's lifelong training as a weightlifter and bodybuilder has enabled her to perform wrestling moves normally reserved for men. Here Chyna tosses her opponent, Eddie Guerrero, during a WrestleMania 2000 match.

guidance. She wanted a new start and thought she could find that with her dad and his new spouse. Laurer wanted to be in an environment that gave her a chance to learn new things and find out who she was and what she wanted to do with her life.

Shortly after moving in with her dad, Laurer took up exercising as one of her hobbies. "I was kicked out of the house when I was 15," Chyna told a magazine reporter. "I had to grow up fast and I started using fitness as my identity. I was doing the Jane Fonda fitness video three times a day. I could see my body developing, and even though my muscles made me seem different on a freakish level to some people, I knew inside it was a cool thing."

The exercise video eventually led to weightlifting, which helped her occupy some of her free time. Around this time, she moved to Europe with her father and stepmother. In 1985 she received a United Nations scholarship to help her finish her high-school education in Spain, where she not only learned Spanish, but also picked up French and German.

But Laurer's interest in bodybuilding caused her some growing pains. The more Laurer worked out, the bigger she got. She became much more muscular than most girls— or boys—her age. Many people, including her parents, weren't used to seeing such a muscular girl. Some even questioned her sexuality.

"I was called a man and a dyke and a lesbian," she explained. "Anything anybody could possibly think of to put me down. It was a time when women just didn't go to the gym to work out. My parents thought that maybe I was a lesbian because I was lifting weights."

"I think the way that I look makes people feel uncomfortable," she said. "People are very cruel. When you don't look like the norm you tend to be ostracized, ridiculed, and criticized."

When Laurer returned to the United States, she accepted a scholarship from the University of Tampa in Florida, where she studied foreign languages. She excelled in college. But before getting her diploma, she longed to return overseas. In her senior year Laurer had the opportunity to study in Spain. She wanted to get back to Europe, and she wanted to spend some time away from the United States, as she had recently learned that her father had taken out loans under her name, leaving her $40,000 in debt.

In 1992, after graduating early from the University of Tampa with a degree in Spanish literature, Laurer joined the Peace Corps. She was assigned to work in Costa Rica, where she put her Spanish skills to work.

When her stint with the Peace Corps was over, Laurer moved in a new direction. For some time she had considered a career as a diplomat or as a Secret Service member. But before rubbing elbows with the diplomats of the world or becoming a female secret agent, Laurer found a profession in bodybuilding.

She loved working out, and she was good at it. While everyone around her was making fun of her because of her size, Laurer kept her focus and drive and went after what she wanted. Her hobby had made her bigger and better physically, and it would lead to bigger and better things professionally. Bodybuilding once again would get her noticed, but this time would be different than her teen years. Now, working out opened doors for her instead of causing her heartache.

BIGGER AND BETTER THINGS

3

Laurer first made a name for herself in the gym where she trained. By word of mouth, the condition of her physique reached the ears of fitness talent scouts, and one by one, they came by to see with their own eyes the woman everyone was talking about.

In 1995 one of Laurer's first breaks was meeting a fitness promoter by the name of Kenny Kassell. He helped her break into the bodybuilding business and later helped her enter the wrestling world. Laurer asked Kassell if he had contacts in the wrestling business, and when Kassell asked why, she explained that she was interested in trying her skills on the mat. Even though Kassell believed his client had a better chance of making a living on the fitness circuit, he was willing to help her follow her interest.

Kassell knew it wouldn't be easy or lucrative for her to break into the male-dominated sport of wrestling, and he explained this to her. Laurer wanted to try anyway. She didn't care that women's wrestling was not taken seriously or that most of the popular women's matches involved mud or Jell-O. She was determined to give it her best effort, and with Kassell in her corner, she believed that she could succeed.

In physique and in attitude, Chyna is unlike any woman before her in the WWF. She has set a new standard of strength and muscular beauty. According to Chyna, "there are beautiful women of all sizes and shapes, and they ought to show [their bodies] more."

At the time, the two largest federations, the WWF and World Championship Wrestling (WCW) weren't looking for women wrestlers. The federations were more interested in women who looked good rather than women who could wrestle well. As a matter of fact, there wasn't a true women's division in either promotion. Now and again women like Sable would take on other females in the ring, but these were glorified mud-matches that had little to do with wrestling and more to do with ratings.

Kassell worked the phones anyway and contacted everyone he knew in the business to try to get Laurer a chance. One of the calls he made was to Randy Powell, the founder of the Professional Girls Wrestling Association (PGWA), who also worked for another entertainment organization known as Special Events. This contact would prove to be a huge one for Laurer, as Powell's North Carolina-based organization not only put on all-women wrestling events, it also created magazines and videos on the sport.

Almost immediately Powell agreed to help train Laurer. He saw the fire in her eyes and the shape she was in. But Powell also knew he was taking a big risk with this muscular woman, as she had never wrestled before and knew nothing about the business. She was a fitness competitor who had a dream to wrestle, and Powell had the challenging task of showing her the ropes and converting her into a grappler.

"It was no easy task, unfortunately," Powell explained in a *WOW* magazine interview. "She knew nothing about wrestling. I wanted to have her train in North Carolina and was seeking financial backing for her room, board and trainers. I found it nearly impossible to find assistance because no one had heard of her, and they weren't impressed with her fitness background. 'Oh a bodybuilder,' they would say and they would just lose all interest."

A lack of funds kept getting in the way of Powell's plan to help Laurer. On another occasion, he wanted Laurer to train at a school run by a woman wrestler named Susan Green, but he couldn't find anyone to help him sponsor her tuition.

Although he was growing frustrated, as his plans kept falling through, Powell never lost faith or sight of what the future could hold for this talented and determined woman. Laurer also never lost hope. She had been through worse times growing up, so these were only minor obstacles in her professional life. Laurer was familiar with adversity. She liked to stare down challenges just to make a point.

Laurer turned many heads in Boston, Massachusetts, when she took the firefighters exam and passed it. "The fire-fighters test was the most challenging event I have ever been exposed to," she said. Laurer took part in another test of sorts in 1996 when she enrolled in a Massachusetts school run by the legendary wrestler, "Killer" Kowalski.

Kowalski was retired from the sport. He trained men and women who wanted to enter the rough and tumble grappling business. Laurer was thrilled to be in his presence. "Killer" had schooled female wrestlers Brittany Brown and Amanda Storm, who went on to prosper in the tough industry.

Laurer didn't know at the time how much this training course would also help her future

Laurer enrolled in a Massachusetts wrestling school run by the legendary "Killer" Kowalski, a 6' 7", 285-pound grappler who was one of wrestling's most dangerous men in the 1960s.

career. She met wrestlers who she would come in contact with later in her life, and who would also help her get her big break in the industry. Her most-noted classmate was none other than Jean-Paul Levesque, aka Hunter Hearst Helmsley or Triple H. He also became her real-life boyfriend when she made it to the WWF.

Kowalski taught and trained her well, and she picked up ring techniques quickly. As she mastered the craft, perfecting moves like the spring elbow smash, she left an impression on her classmates and teacher.

"She was always hard-working and very pleasant to be around. Joanie has a great sense of humor, but when she gets down to work, her attitude is a kick-butt, no joking style," Kowalski explained.

Laurer was eager to test her newly acquired skills, and it wasn't long before she had a chance.

In 1996 Laurer flew to Las Vegas to attend a women's wrestling convention. She hoped to make some contacts to help her career along. Accompanying her was her number one supporter, Randy Powell, who was going to work every angle and contact he knew in order to get Laurer on the women's wrestling map.

The duo worked the convention like an in-sync tag team. Powell introduced Laurer as one of the PGWA's up-and-coming stars, and she obliged by showing off her physique and mingling with promoters and media types.

This turned out to be a perfect fit for Laurer, as she enjoyed being around the people of the wrestling world and loved the attention and hype she received. As Powell recalled, each and every person she interacted with took an immediate liking to her. She was a natural, and she was becoming a pro almost overnight.

"As I introduced Joanie to those in attendance, people knew she was a real pro wrestler and not just a wanna-be who had crashed the convention," he said.

But Powell knew that this was only the beginning. While Laurer was a hit outside the ring, she had yet to set foot between the ropes in live competition. In order for their trip to Vegas to truly be a success, Powell knew he had to get Laurer a match.

The PGWA founder wanted nothing more than for Laurer to get a chance at some live action. He had promoters running away from him because he had asked them to include Laurer on their wrestling card so many times. But then he ran into Lillian Ellison, the president of a women's division called the Ladies International Wrestling Association (LIWA).

Ellison, whose ring name was the Fabulous Moolah, was one of wrestling's greatest-ever female stars. Several times she turned down Powell's pleas to add his girl to her card. She had every right to ignore his suggestions, as she had a reputation to uphold in the business. "I had offered Lillian the chance to have Joanie on the live card they held at the convention, but she declined," he said. "Of course, who could blame her for saying no? No one except me knew who Joanie was, what she could do, or if she could handle a pro match."

Eventually Ellison came around and agreed to use Laurer in one of her matches in Las Vegas. Laurer's first match would be against another rookie, Angie Jenet. Powell managed to work out a sweet deal for his protégé, for if she beat Jenet, she would have the opportunity to take part in another match at the convention. This was just what she wanted, as Powell's arrangement had her taking part in a mixed tag team match, with other men and women, if she won her first bout.

The Jenet/Laurer match was memorable for both of the new wrestlers. Laurer beat Jenet convincingly, and she broke her opponent's nose in the match. While this must have been a painful experience for Jenet, she now had the distinction of being the future-Chyna's first opponent.

"Joanie was the star of the show," Powell said. "Every fan loved the match she had. Angie

Jenet was Joanie's opponent, and I am sure Jenet will always be proud of this match. Angie was also a talented rookie, but she couldn't match Joanie's strength and ended up breaking her nose. She put up a good fight, but Joanie won the match."

Laurer moved on to the mixed tag team match that night. She and her male partner came out victorious, making the rookie 2–0 in her mat debut. The crowd cheered her, and she was now on her way to making a name for herself on the pro wrestling circuit. Speaking of names, Laurer had to pick a moniker to go by in the wrestling business. She decided on Joanie Lee.

Laurer was way too powerful for the female foes she encountered in the early stages of her career. She usually disposed of her competitors in lightning quick fashion, since they couldn't match her size and talents in the ring.

As she learned the ropes under Powell and the PGWA, Laurer also brought in money for the Special Events organization that sold videos and magazines featuring the rookie grappler.

The fans took to Laurer quickly. She was bigger in size than the other women wrestlers she faced. She also had a different in-ring personality than she has today. Wrestling as "Joanie Lee," Laurer dressed as an all-American woman with blond hair. She wore a red, white, and blue outfit and wrestled by the rules. In the beginning of her career, she knew no other way to tackle and beat her opponents except by the book. She not only wanted to win her matches, she wanted to prove that she didn't need gimmicks or foreign objects to take down her foes. This plan worked well for the muscular bomber,

One of Laurer's classmates at Kowalski's school was Jean-Paul Levesque, center, known as Hunter Hearst Helmsley, or Triple H, in the WWF. In 1997 when Triple H invited Laurer to become his bodyguard, she took on the persona of Chyna and often interfered in his matches, helping him subdue opponents like the Undertaker.

as she had the size and strength to defeat anyone on the circuit without any aid.

In the fall of 1996 Laurer altered her approach and philosophy in the ring when she found out the hard way that not everyone likes to play by the rules. Laurer had made her way south to work for the Universal Wrestling Federation (UWF). The promotion had two female stars at the time: Riptide and Liz Chase. Almost immediately Laurer and Riptide formed a heated rivalry. Laurer found out that the UWF women were notorious for breaking bones and rules. She soon discovered that it was either kill or be killed in the UWF, so she fought fire with fire.

The most memorable match between Laurer and her rival Riptide came at the Iron Horse Saloon in Daytona Beach, Florida, while Special Events was there taping a video called Wild Women at the Iron Horse. Both female grapplers lived up to the wild women title, as they went at each other tooth and (manicured) nails.

This was the first time that Laurer was up against a formidable foe. Riptide was unlike any competitor she had met up until this point in her career. Riptide was not in the business for her looks. She was a legitimate wrestler who came from a shootfighting background, and like Laurer, she also had bodybuilding credentials.

But even with her rulebreaking ways, chiseled physique, and wide array of maneuvers, Riptide still came out on the losing end against Laurer. It was definitely the best matchup to this point in Laurer's career. She even had to learn an illegal trick or two. In the end, Laurer's arms were raised in victory.

This victory and style change helped Laurer earn PGWA Rookie of the Year honors in 1996, and she seemed destined for stardom. As for her rule bending, she had this to say: "Everyone was breaking the rules, and I just saw a reason to fight fire with fire."

Even though she was happy to earn the Rookie of the Year honor, Laurer wanted more. She knew that she had what it took to defeat any other female wrestler, but that's not what she was looking for. She wanted a chance to make it on the men's circuit. She wanted to be able to beat anyone standing—male or female.

So Laurer's next step was to add some more weapons to her already lethal arsenal. She took up boxing and karate. She wanted to improve her hand and eye coordination as well as her strength. Determined to be the best, Laurer quietly turned herself into a one woman wrecking crew.

Taking up karate and boxing gave Laurer the extra edge she needed to get to the next level. She no longer relied on the people in her promotions to get her work. She took her career into her own hands. In one instance she publicly challenged Madusa, one of the female wrestlers from WCW, to a match, but the bold battler was turned down.

Laurer didn't stop there! When she had no luck challenging women, she took the next logical step and started calling out men! When no man dared to answer her call, she decided to go after them.

One night while doing a television appearance for the American Independent Wrestling Federation (AIWF) wrestling show, she presented her challenge to one of the male wrestlers on the show, "Bad" Brad. At the time, Brad laughed off her challenge, but he wasn't laughing a couple of hours later.

When Laurer's female opponent didn't show up for the match, Brad decided to take her place. Laurer not only won the match that night, she left Brad wondering if he had gotten hit by a truck. She attacked him with everything she had, and it was more than enough to defeat "Bad" Brad. She worked him over, beat him from pillar to post, and made Brad look about as "bad" as any male wrestler has ever looked in the ring.

These independent show victories were all good for Laurer, but she yearned for the big time. Yes, she was making progress against the best on the indy circuit, but she wanted to square off against the best of the best on the pro circuit. And she now had a taste of what it was like to face a man in the ring and defeat him. Laurer prayed now more than ever for a shot at the big show.

4

THE WWF
COMES CALLING

Laurer's prayers were answered in 1997 when one of her wrestling school classmates, Hunter Hearst Helmsley (Triple H), who was now wrestling for the WWF, asked if she was interested in joining him.

Triple H wanted her to join him as his personal bodyguard and escort him into the arena before his matches. Unlike the other male wrestlers, Helmsley wanted a woman as his bodyguard. He also wanted someone who could truly back him up in times of need.

It didn't take Laurer long to say yes to Helmsley. From there she climbed the ladder of success. She was eased into the WWF picture, first coming onto the scene at ringside during Helmsley's matches, where she watched and cheered her former classmate.

Laurer got her first taste of the WWF spotlight at a February 16, 1997, match in Chattanooga, Tennessee, between Helmsley and Rocky Maivia for the intercontinental belt. Goldust and his valet Marlena interfered in the contest, causing Helmsley to lose the match. Laurer jumped out of her seat to aid her friend. She manhandled Goldust's five-foot-tall sidekick and won the crowd over, as well as Helmsley.

Triple H officially introduced her to the audience at WrestleMania in 1997 as his new bodyguard and partner in

WWF guest referee Jesse Ventura points to Triple H's bodyguard, Chyna, and lays down the law during a SummerSlam match on August 22, 1999, at the Target Center in Minneapolis, Minnesota. Ventura removed Chyna from the match because of her constant interference.

crime, Chyna. Even though it was a long, hard road to acceptance from the audience and her peers from there, Chyna took it all in stride. She broke down walls and barriers as they came along and made a name for herself in a short time.

Soon she was in the ring taking on big-time wrestlers like "Stone Cold" Steve Austin, Goldust, and The Undertaker. In 1997 she became a founding member of the trouble-causing gang of wrestlers known as D-Generation X. This association was key for her because they became so popular with the fans at the time of their creation, the gang was in the spotlight each and every week, giving Chyna more exposure. And the fact that she was the only female member of the posse made her stand out even more.

Chyna quickly gained a reputation as a bully on the male-dominated wrestling circuit. Her now jet-black hair and outfits showed her dark side to the wrestling world. She thrived in her time in the limelight and her character seemed to grow more and more popular with each passing week. The crowd loved the antics of Chyna and the other members of D-Generation X: Helmsley, Shawn Michaels, Road Dogg, and X-Pac.

Chyna was surprised when D-Generation X became so popular with wrestling fans, and she was grateful for the opportunity to showcase her talent in the WWF. "It was Hunter [Hearst Helmsley] and Shawn Michaels who thought of this really hip 90's idea of having a female bodyguard," she said, "and I think the two of them really really pushed for it, which finally got me in the door, and I think that the first

A founding member of the rulebreaking clique known as D-Generation X, Chyna, shown with Dxers Shawn Michaels, center, and Triple H, right, quickly earned a reputation as a bully.

time I went out there it really took off. It could have gone either way. I was very pleased."

As a new WWF phenomenon, Chyna took advantage of every opportunity that came her way. When D-Generation X disbanded she really got to show off for the audience and the other wrestlers. She had gotten her start with Triple H and D-Generation X, but her time to shine individually was upon her, and she didn't want to let the opportunity slip through her fingers.

"What I really think people want to see is a woman like me kicking some guys' butts," Chyna

said. "To me, the [federation women] are a bunch
of bimbos wrestling around. I am far beyond that
and in a completely different category."

In 1999 Chyna rewrote the federation's
record books when she became the first female
wrestler to take part in both the Royal Rumble
and the King of the Ring tournament. Chyna
qualified for the Royal Rumble in impressive
fashion when she launched WWF head honcho

*Chyna's valet and
diminutive look-alike,
Miss Kitty, left, was
once employed by
Chyna's foe Jeff
Jarrett.*

Vince McMahon Jr. over the top rope one evening to gain the 30th and final spot in the tourney.

On October 17, 1999, Chyna squared off against mat veteran Jeff Jarrett at a No Mercy event in Cleveland, Ohio. She beat her opponent in a "Good Housekeeping" match and walked away with the WWF Intercontinental title around her waist. This marked the first time in wrestling history that a female held a male's championship belt. At this point in her career, she also introduced the wrestling world to her new valet, Miss Kitty, who was not only Jarrett's former employee, but also a mini-version of Chyna. Kitty entered the ring at Chyna's side decked out in jet-black hair and formfitting black leather outfits.

Chyna held onto the title for almost two months. During that time, she became acquainted with wrestler Mark Henry. She also went corporate for a while, joining forces with Vince McMahon Jr. and the Corporation, which led to a public spat with her one-time confidant, Triple H. Little by little, she was working her way to the top, as evidenced by her "getting down" with Rikishi and Too Cool in the middle of the ring on some nights.

Chyna's first intercontinental reign came to an end when she met up with "the Lionheart" Chris Jericho and faced him at Armageddon on December 12, 1999, in Fort Lauderdale, Florida. Jericho defeated her for the title. By now Chyna was not only getting the respect she deserved from her fellow wrestlers, she was also growing popular with the fans, who voted her Diva of the Year for 1999.

In 2000 Chyna picked up right where she left off. Only three days into the new year she won her second intercontinental title at a match in Miami, Florida. Even though she had to share the belt with Chris Jericho because of an in-ring controversy sparked by Stephanie McMahon-Helmsley, she didn't care, as long as she had the belt around her waist and the title to her credit.

Twenty days later Chyna faced off against Jericho for the intercontinental belt, but this time it wasn't just the two wrestlers going at one another. This was a Triple Threat match, and Chyna had to face "the Lionheart" as well as Hardcore Holly. In the end, Jericho came out the victor, but again Chyna didn't care, as she held her own against her two opponents.

Chyna, whom some people were now calling "The Ninth Wonder of the World," started an association with Eddie Guerrero and helped the Latin brawler find success on the WWF circuit. Before she became the apple of his eye, the two wrestlers were constantly at each other's throats.

At WrestleMania 2000 in California, Chyna wrestled Guerrero in a match that included Too Cool on her side and Perry Saturn and Dean Malenko on his. Guerrero cheap-shotted Chyna every chance he got, but the female grappler got her revenge on him that night, as she cheap-shotted him back and got the win.

Chyna and Guerrero faced off again at SummerSlam 2000 when they both took part in a four-way match with Trish Stratus and Val Venis for the WWF Intercontinental title. This was a stipulation match where any wrestler to get a pin would come away with the title. In the end Chyna got the victory and earned her third intercontinental belt. This accomplishment is

Eddie Guerrero battles Chyna in the ring. Guerrero tried to woo Chyna by bringing her a dozen red roses each night before their matches, but she decided she didn't need him in her life.

impressive in itself, as many male grapplers go their entire careers without winning this belt once, let alone three times.

A couple of weeks later, on September 4, 2000, Guerrero won the belt from Chyna. Guerrero then started bringing Chyna a dozen red roses each night before their matches. He tried to make Chyna like him by being sweet to her. Twenty days later Chyna assisted

Chyna slaps Chris Jericho during their match for the I-C title on January 23, 2000, at the Royal Rumble. Chyna lost the match to Jericho.

Guerrero in his title-defense over the well-rounded wrestler Rikishi. Even though her interference infuriated Rikishi, it made Guerrero fonder of Chyna.

In one of the WWF plots, the two became "engaged" later in the year, but all did not remain beautiful in paradise. The last straw of their relationship came when Chyna threw her ring back in Guerrero's face and accused him of being unfaithful to her. Chyna couldn't be bothered with a cheating heart, so she left Guerrero to concentrate on her one real true love—wrestling.

This was bad news for Guerrero and the rest of the wrestlers on the WWF circuit. They knew that when Chyna put her heart, mind, body, and soul into something, there was no limit as to what the Ninth Wonder of the World could accomplish. Jim Ross, a WWF ring announcer with 25 years of experience in the business, called her "the best female athlete I have ever seen in this business."

Speaking of her career prospects, Chyna said, "I refuse to be pinned down."

5

A DAY IN THE LIFE
OF A PRO WRESTLER

Most people usually follow the same routine when they get up for work in the morning. A typical day might be to wake up about two hours before work, then shower, maybe have a little breakfast, and then hop on the bus or train to make the daily trek into the office.

But unlike the everyday nine-to-fiver, Chyna has to face the mornings with a new agenda each time. There really is no typical day in the life of a pro wrestler.

"There's no such thing as a typical day in the WWF," she said. "It's an extreme circus. I don't even know how to explain it sometimes. It's a freak show and I love it!"

Even though their plots are scripted in the ring, each day brings a new challenge to the wrestlers. Chyna's days could start at 5 a.m. if she has to make an appearance on a morning talk show to promote an upcoming event or travel to another city. She conditioned herself to be prepared for anything both inside and outside the wrestling stage.

"You've got to be on your toes ready to go because you never know what's going to happen," she said on MTV's *Diary*. "There's just so much going on. Sometimes you don't have anything to do and you're waiting with anticipation to find out what's going to happen that night."

Chyna never knows what each new day in the WWF will bring. She is never afraid to put her fitness to the test and has even challenged her former employer Triple H to a little one-on-one in the ring.

Even though she loves what she's doing, she's also aware that she's just one of the many players in the WWF organization. "I often think to myself that I'm a woman who's broken all these boundaries, but ultimately, I'm just this piece of property that's being used to go out and sell this product."

And sell she does. It's not unheard of for Chyna to be on the road for a month at a time, weekdays and weekends, calling the hotels around the world home.

Like the other WWF wrestlers, she does 280 shows a year—television shows, house shows, and arena shows. Chyna and the other wrestlers are on the road for 280 days with no seasonal breaks or vacations during that time. On top of this gruelling schedule, there are injuries that come with the job. Chyna has had a broken tailbone, recurrent back, neck, and knee trouble, and she has undergone shoulder surgery as a result of injuries sustained on the job.

Despite her size and strength, Chyna could not ignore the impact that wrestling had on her body. "Whether or not you want to think about what we do as choreographed," she said, "it definitely takes an athlete to do what we are doing. Yes I portray this bad, butt-kicking woman, but the guys outweigh me by a hundred pounds or more. When they hot you, throw you around, or land on you, it's that much more of a strain on my body than it is on them."

"The traveling is probably the most difficult part of this job because it never ends," she explained. Sure, before she made it big she knew that the wrestlers traveled from city to city for events, but she never imagined how hard or lonely life would be away from home. Over time, she learned to adjust.

"When I first started here I thought I would never last a day. I couldn't travel on the road," she said. "I used to cry. It was very difficult by myself, but now I couldn't imagine being without these guys." As Chyna pointed out, it wasn't always easy. "Being away from your family. Not having as much time for friends. I feel lonely sometimes and that makes me really sad. I guess maybe that's overanalyzing it, but you just try to go with the flow."

Chyna was not sad for long. The chiseled bomber was grateful to Vince McMahon and the opportunity he gave her. She wouldn't trade places with anyone in the world. "Vince didn't want me at first," Chyna recalled. "But after talking to him for about four or five months, he said he would give me a try. He put 100 percent support behind me and that in itself is a reward for my 30 years of hard work."

"Vince McMahon to me in a way is my quasi-stepfather. Vince was the first person who really gave me an opportunity. You deal with him a lot. Sometimes I absolutely love him and adore him as a person and sometimes I'd like to kick him too," she joked.

Even though she is forever grateful, sometimes her body yearns for a break. "The schedule is not for the lazy. Your body never gets a rest. We're traveling from east coast to west coast [and] I think it would be more difficult for me to do if I hated what I do. But I love what I do."

Chyna's love for the sport was tested when she traveled from city to city. She found out the hard way that there was no privacy in the

Chyna has compared her life in the WWF to traveling with the circus. Though she enjoys her fame, she sometimes finds the demands of her public life overwhelming. She misses her privacy— as well as her family and friends—when she is on the road.

wrestling/celebrity business. "I think sometimes if I have to pick up my happy suitcase one more time, I'm going to break. Privacy is definitely nonexistent for me at this point."

No matter what time of day or night she arrives at an airport or in a hotel, she is always hounded for pictures and autographs. "It's difficult at 12:00 at night and there's people there expecting that you give them an autograph or a picture. I'm not made up 24 hours a day and I don't want to have my picture shown somewhere that I'm not looking my best.

I'm a human being and I think that people forget that sometimes."

She regretted not being able to sign autographs for everyone. She wished she could sign an autograph for each person who approached her, but on the other hand, sometimes she just wanted her privacy. "You feel bad because you know on one hand you don't want to turn people down, but on the other hand, it's an invasion of privacy. Your home is the hotel on the road. I don't think people know I've been traveling all day long and seeing people at the airports all day, and at the store, and at the restaurant, and everywhere. It's hard to be nice 24 hours a day."

Chyna does not find it difficult to separate her in-ring personality from her real self, but she says that sometimes other people do. "You know, it's not like I am playing a doctor on TV—and when I go home people know I am just playing a doctor—people see me as Chyna on the street, and when I go to a restaurant to eat, they still see me as Chyna."

Fans expect pro wrestlers to be the same people they play on TV, but this is not often the case.

As Chyna herself admits, her ring character is very different from the real-life Joanie Laurer. "Chyna is so opposite from Joanie it makes me laugh when I think about it—because Joanie is probably one of the most sensitive, silly, feminine women you would ever meet."

Even though she sometimes finds it hard to live the life of a pro wrestler, when it is time to enter the ring and perform, Chyna martials the energy to take on any and all challenges, or challengers, in her case!

"When I first started, I used to get nervous just to be there—just to be at the building," she said. "Now, I'm much more nervous on a performance level. Even after four years of doing this, the bar is constantly raised and therefore my performance has to be better. I might be tired that day, but I have to be right on [and] ready to go."

"Around four or five o'clock, I start getting down to business now for my wrestling match. I start to figure out what I'm going to do and go over maybe a couple of big moves that we do. Right before I go out I'll forget everything and I'll go into a complete panic. I get really petrified (and) nervous. I wring my hands a lot."

"(But) as soon as I walk out of that curtain I don't know what happens, but that light just switches on. There is absolutely nothing like that reaction of thousands of screaming fans. And you go out and people get up out of their seats and they're yelling and screaming. That's an incredible adrenaline rush."

Chyna has had many "firsts" in pro wrestling. In addition to being the only woman currently competing against men in the WWF, she was the first woman to capture a men's WWF title, the first woman to compete in a Royal Rumble pay per view, and the first woman to battle WWF male superstars like "Stone Cold" Steve Austin, Triple-H, and Kane. So it was no surprise when *Jane* magazine gave Chyna their "Gutsiest Athlete" award in 2000.

Chyna has said many times that she has no interest in pursuing a WWF women's wrestling title, as it would not be much of a challenge for her. She knows that she is in a class by herself and that there are no worthy female opponents for her to beat. Until that changes, she plans to keep going after the men's titles and to continue competing in male-dominated events—hopefully against the federation's top-tier wrestlers.

Chyna has enjoyed her roles as both an athlete and an entertainer in the WWF, but the downside is that with such a demanding work and travel schedule, she doesn't seem to have time for a personal life. Her job and the WWF come first, and all else second.

"You can't take time for personal issues," she said. "The show must go on and I must go on."

6 BREAKING DOWN THE WALLS OF CHYNA

The popularity of professional wrestling at the turn of the millennium helped create a climate in which a woman with Chyna's skills could succeed. When asked why people were tuning in to WWF television shows, Chyna said, "I think earlier people were so focused on whether it [wrestling] was fake or weather it was real—people weren't just accepting it for what it is—and that is excellent sports entertainment."

Chyna was able to parlay her interests in fitness and body-building and her love of acting into a solid wrestling career. She has not only made a name for herself between the ropes, she has also become popular away from the arena, gracing the covers of mainstream magazines like *Playboy* and *Newsweek* and appearing on TV shows such as *Live with Regis and Kathie Lee*, *Third Rock from the Sun*, and *Pacific Blue*. The ring queen appeared at the 2000 Democratic National Convention in order to promote the WWF's Smackdown Your Vote voter registration campaign and helped secure over 60,000 new voters with her efforts. "Politics really intimidated me for a long time," she admitted before saying "but you do have a say in what happens in your future." Another WWF wrestler, the Rock, aka Dwayne Johnson, made a similar

---

Chyna appeared at the 2000 Democratic National Convention in Los Angeles and encouraged young people, who typically have the lowest voter turnout rates, to register to vote.

appeal to young voters at the 2000 Republican National Convention in Philadelphia.

"I think by doing the things that I have done on television and by posing for *Playboy* magazine, I've really broken the ice for a lot of other women to look how they want to look," Laurer said.

"I originally wanted to be a movie star, but because I was always very big physically, that wasn't really possible for me. So I started wrestling because I thought it would be my niche, and it was."

By appearing in *Playboy*, Chyna took a huge leap, as she doesn't consider her body shape to be of the kind usually featured in this magazine. "It's a powerful statement," she said of her appearance in the popular men's magazine. "There haven't been a lot of women in *Playboy* who look like I do. I am not the norm for beauty. But this is who I am and this is beautiful."

And the woman with 14-inch biceps who could bench press 365 pounds is totally satisfied with where she is today. "I'm finally in a place where I've always wanted to be and how I've always wanted to be looked at," she said in an interview in the November 2000 issue of *Raw* magazine.

The New York native always wanted to be able to keep her size and her femininity without anyone questioning either, and she feels she's achieved that. "I don't think I necessarily represent a bodybuilder's body. It's not what I'm after. I consider my body to be more statuesque— compare it to a Greek statue instead of a huge, muscle-bound woman."

Aside from the fact that Chyna was the first woman to beat a male opponent in the ring and

Chyna, center, stands with fellow DXers Shawn Michaels and Triple-H, whom she credits for helping her get her start in the WWF.

win a championship title, the WWF ring queen has also made other noteworthy appearances outside the ropes.

The grappling beauty was also a presenter at 2000's MTV Video Awards, where she gave away an award with a little help from Richard Hatch, the winner from the hit TV show *Survivor*. Chyna made quite an impression that evening when she appeared in a Wonder Woman outfit that showed off her awesome body. She also manhandled her copresenter in front of millions of viewers.

The WWF's leading lady also made several television appearances on prime time TV and talk shows in 2000. She made a guest appearance on *The Tonight Show* with Jay Leno, where she impressed the talk show host with her wit, charm, and muscular build.

"I very much enjoy doing the talk shows," she explained. "It's fun. It rewards you for being

Looking like Wonder Woman, Chyna arrives at the 2000 MTV Video Music Awards on September 7, 2000, at Radio City Music Hall in New York.

a star. It feels really great to go on these shows and be recognized for all the very special things that you do."

In 2000, Chyna also appeared on the NBC sitcom *Third Rock from the Sun*, starring John Lithgow and Jane Curtain. Her character was that of a police officer whom everybody constantly wanted to pick a fight with. Her character went over so well that the show's writers created a recurring role for her for the rest of the season. *The National Enquirer*, which usually has negative articles, had glowing words for the WWF wrestler's acting skills. They wrote: "Chyna should be her own character in a TV series. She should be the next female Terminator; she should be Wonder Woman 2000." Not a bad review for a bone-crusher turned actress!

Chyna also appeared on the police drama *Pacific Blue* in the year 2000. She followed in the footsteps of another female wrestling personality, Rena Mero, aka Sable, who also appeared on the television show. Laurer's real-life boyfriend and coworker, Triple H, also had a guest spot on the show. But unlike Sable and Triple H, Chyna's safecracking/bodybuilding character was well received by the audience. The critics were much nicer to Chyna than they were to her two predecessors.

Chyna also made an appearance on MTV's *Time Out* and MTV's *Diary*. She then moved from the small screen to the big screen when she took on a role in the sci-fi thriller *Alien Fury: Countdown to Invasion*.

Chyna's success hasn't only been in the ring or on the screen. The WWF's "Wonder Woman" also had her own comic book put out by

CHAOS! Comics. Called *Chyna*, the comic features the wrestler performing in the future. She also shows some emotion too. It is sort of a modern-day version of the Wonder Woman female super hero of DC Comic and television series fame, but with a wrestling flare. Speaking about her comic book, Chyna said she was very happy with the outcome because she always felt that Chyna was a larger-than-life female with a larger-than-life physique who could go out and beat up all these guys with no problem.

Another project of which she is very proud is her fitness video, *Chyna Fitness: More Than Meets the Eye*, which was released in September 2000. The video is a 40-minute circuit-training program designed for anyone who is serious about getting physically fit.

Chyna Fitness includes a thorough warm-up routine of basic boxing maneuvers like jabs, hooks, jump rope, and squats. The program is like a simulated boxing match, where you train for six rounds, with each round containing three minutes of strength training with weights, one minute of cardio workout, and one minute of stretching.

The back cover of the video summed it up best: "*Chyna Fitness* isn't about having the biggest guns or the tightest buns. It's about what makes you feel and look your best. I've worked really hard to get this body and people are always asking me how I do it."

Chyna Fitness not only shows the viewers how she got her chiseled body, it also takes the consumers right into Chyna's workout room, where they can experience their makeover together with the WWF star. "They figure I spend my life in the gym. Well, most days I'm traveling from one area to the next. I've come up with a routine I can do anywhere, that makes the most of my time. It works, it's fun, and I'll be sweating right along with you."

With help from author Michael Angeli, Chyna also penned her autobiography, *Chyna: If They Only Knew*, which was scheduled for release in January 2001. In the book Chyna explains how she became the successful, strong person she is today.

Chyna's road to the ring was not an easy one. Along the way, she redefined the role of women in professional wrestling and set new standards of female beauty. She overcame personal barriers before she knocked down the professional barriers she encountered in the wrestling world. And once she overcame these obstacles, there was no stopping her!

QUOTEWORTHY:
Chyna on Chyna

CHYNA'S IDEAL MAN . . .

"I do have to have a physically fit man. He has to take care of himself. I'm attracted to larger men because I always wonder 'if he hugs me, will he be able to reach all the way around my back?'"

CHYNA ON EATING . . .

"As for eating, I believe in moderation," she says. "But if I want to have a piece of cheesecake on Friday night because I love it, then I absolutely do. And I put the raspberry sauce and whipped cream on it too! And I have a cappuccino to boot. That's what makes it all worth it!"

CHYNA ON WEIGHT TRAINING . . .

"It's not how much you train or how often you train, it's the intensity. Every time I go to the gym I give 110 percent. I don't work out more than an hour. If I work as hard as I can I'm going to be spent in 40 minutes."

CHYNA ON THE ORIGIN OF HER RING NAME . . .

"They came up with it for me [the WWF officials]; it's a very boring story. We chose "Chyna" because we thought it was the opposite of what I represent. It's delicate-sounding, and I am this big, powerful woman. So, I'm more like the bull in the Chyna shop."

CHYNA ON JOBS SHE'S HELD BEFORE WRESTLING . . .

"Just about everything you could think of, from singing telegrams to selling beepers. I've done it all."

CHYNA ON THE PRESSURE FOR HER TO PERFORM IN THE WWF . . .

"I couldn't go in the ring and fight these guys if I was five-foot-five and didn't really have the strength to back up my fighting. I have to go out in the ring—which is our stage—in front of anywhere from 20,000 to 50,000 people and I have to get it right the first time because there's not a second chance."

CHYNA'S REGRETS . . .

"I don't think I have any regrets. All of my experiences have made me the person I am today. I still get frustrated at times because women still have a long way to go, but I think we're finally getting there."

CHYNA ON THE FUTURE . . .

"I'm not laying down tomorrow. I've worked extremely hard to be in the position I'm in. It's sort of a difficult question to say where am I going to be—what does my future hold professionally and personally—because it's not a very normal life that I lead."

"I want a husband and I would love to have a family one day," she explained in *Playboy*. "But I'm not going to be the kind of woman who's at home with the kids. I'd put my baby on my hip and go do a movie. I'm a go-getter and that's what makes my life exciting."

CHYNA ON THE WWF HEAVYWEIGHT CHAMPIONSHIP . . .

"I would love to be world champion. I don't know if the world is ready for a female champion, but if there was one, I would like it to be me. It wouldn't matter who I fought; it would be more the principle of holding the title."

JOANIE LAURER ON CHYNA . . .

"Chyna is just one facet of Joanie. However, 90 percent of my life is taken over by Chyna [and] what she does."

CHYNA ON HER APPEARANCE . . .

"It has been so very difficult for the public to accept my physique, and I've been so proud that I have made it to where I have made it . . . even being 20 pounds heavier . . . but it's still really really tough marketability wise to get into other avenues when you are a big woman."

CHYNA ON WORKING OUT . . .

"It's really tough with our schedule . . . we're on the road about 280 days out of the year, but when we can it usually ends up being about 3 or 4 times a week, 2 hours a day, and I give it 100 percent."

CHYNA ON BEING A PIONEER . . .

"You know every day I am so thankful to be doing what I am because I feel that I am really a pioneer as a female to be in this completely male-dominated entertainment field . . . I look around me and think 'Gosh, I am in the middle of this ring with all these guys and I'm holding my own.' "

Chronology

1970   Born in Rochester, New York, on December 27

1985   Receives high school scholarship to study abroad in Europe

1992   Graduates from the University of Tampa and joins the Peace Corps

1995   Meets fitness promoter Kenny Kassell, who helps her break into bodybuilding and the wrestling industry; meets Randy Powell, founder of the PGWA

1996   Enrolls in Killer Kowalski's wrestling school; meets fellow wrestlers Triple H and Perry Saturn; attends women's wrestling convention and wrestles in her first pro match of her career against Angie Jenet; wrestles in the UWF and PGWA; wins Rookie of the Year honors

1997   First enters the WWF scene at an In Your House event featuring Hunter Hearst Helmsley and Rocky Maivia; is introduced to the wrestling audience as Chyna, the bodyguard for Triple H; becomes a founding member of D-Generation X

1999   Becomes the first woman to take part in the Royal Rumble and the King of the Ring tournament; wins the WWF Intercontinental championship from male foe Jeff Jarrett; is voted wrestling's Diva of the Year

2000   Wins her second WWF Intercontinental championship; teams with Too Cool against Eddie Guerrero, Perry Saturn and Dean Malenko at WrestleMania; wrestles at SummerSlam in a four-way match with Trish Stratus, Val Venis, and Eddie Guerrero and wins her third WWF Intercontinental championship; appears at the Democratic National Convention; releases a fitness video, *Chyna Fitness*; appears on MTV's *Diary*

2001   Publishes a book, *Chyna: If They Only Knew*

Further Reading

Edelman, Scott. *Warrior Queen.* New York: Ballantine Books, 2000.

Fazioli, Mike. "Strength and Sensuality." *Raw* (November 2000): 30–35.

Greenberg, Keith Elliot. "Wonder Woman." *Raw* (March 2000): 30–39.

Laurer, Joanie, and Michael Angeli. *Chyna: If They Only Knew.* New York: Regan Books, 2001.

Picarello, Rob. *Wrestling's Heels and Heroes.* St. Louis: Boulevard, 2001.

Index

Austin, Steve, 32, 46

Brown, Brittany, 21

Chase, Liz, 26

Chyna
  becomes bodyguard
    for Triple H, 31
  childhood, 13–17
  enrolls in wrestling
    school, 21
  joins D-Generation X, 32
  makes wrestling debut, 24
  signs with WWF, 31
  wins WWF Intercontinental
    title, 11, 35, 36
  wrestles with UWF, 26

Chyna Fitness, 54

Chyna: If They Only Knew,
  55

D-Generation X, 32, 33

Ellison, Lillian, 24

Fabulous Moolah, the,
  7, 24

Goldust, 31, 32

Green, Susan, 21

Guerrero, Eddie, 36–38

Henry, Mark, 35

Jarrett, Jeff, 10, 35

Jenet, Angie, 24, 25

Jericho, Chris, 35, 36

Kane, 46

Kassell, Kenny, 19, 20

Kowalski, Killer, 21–23

Laurer, Joanie. *See Chyna.*

Madusa, 28

Malenko, Dean, 36

Marlena, 8

McMahon, Stephanie, 36

McMahon, Vince, Jr., 10,
  35, 43

Michaels, Shawn, 32

Miss Kitty, 35

Powell, Randy, 20–25

Profesional Girls Wrestling
  Association, 20, 23, 25, 27

Rikishi, 35, 38

Riptide, 26, 27

Road Dogg, 32

Rock, the, 31, 49

Ross, Jim, 39

Sable, 8, 53

Saturn, Perry, 36

Storm, Amanda, 21

Stratus, Trish, 36

Too Cool, 35, 36

Triple H, 8, 22, 31–33,
  35, 46, 53

Undertaker, the, 32

Venis, Val, 36

X-Pac, 32

Young, Mae, 7

Photo Credits

The Acci'Dent: pp. 2, 15, 37, 40, 51, 56, 60; Associated Press/WWP: pp. 30, 52;
Bettmann/Corbis: p. 22; Jeff Eisenberg Sports Photography: pp. 12, 18, 33, 34,
38; Howard Kernats Photography: pp. 6, 8, 9, 44, 48; Sports Action: p. 26.

JOHANNA BRINDISI is a native New Yorker who was born and raised in Monticello to Marie and William Brindisi. Johanna became interested in wrestling after watching her dad, "Willy Love," perform in the ring for several independent federations in the Metropolitan area. Although "Love" never won a title in his brief career, he became popular with the local fans, as he was always escorted to the arena by a harem of beautiful ladies. While she loved watching her dad work the ropes, she never aspired to put on the tights. Instead she decided to go behind the scenes and write about the wrestling industry. In her spare time, Johanna also writes poetry and fiction. She is an avid skydiver and mountain climber, and her two best friends in the world are her dog Bandit and her pet monkey Kong, named after the Hall of Fame wrestler, "King Kong" Bundy.